# DESTROYING ETHNIC IDENTITY:
# THE TURKS OF GREECE

August 1990

A Helsinki Watch Report

Human Rights Watch
485 Fifth Avenue
New York, NY 10017
Tel. (212) 972-8400
Fax (212) 972-0905

Human Rights Watch
1522 K Street, NW, #910
Washington, DC 20005
Tel. (202) 371-6592
Fax (202) 371-0124

(c) August 1990 by Human Rights Watch
All rights reserved.
Printed in the United States of America

ISBN 0-929692-70-5
Library of Congress Catalogue Card Number: 90-84212

## HELSINKI WATCH

Helsinki Watch was established in 1979 to monitor and promote observance of internationally-recognized human rights in the Helsinki signatory countries. The Chairman of Helsinki Watch is Robert L. Bernstein; Vice Chairmen are Jonathan Fanton and Alice Henkin; Executive Director is Jeri Laber; Deputy Director is Lois Whitman; Washington Representative is Catherine Cosman; Staff Counsel are Holly Cartner and Theodore Zang, Jr.

## HUMAN RIGHTS WATCH

Human Rights Watch is composed of five Watch Committees: Africa Watch, Americas Watch, Asia Watch, Helsinki Watch, and Middle East Watch.

Executive Committee: Robert L. Bernstein, Chairman; Adrian W. DeWind, Vice Chairman; Roland Algrant; Lisa Anderson; Peter Bell; Dorothy Cullman; Jonathan Fanton; Jack Greenberg; Alice H. Henkin; Stephen Kass; Marina Kaufman; Jeri Laber; Aryeh Neier; Bruce Rabb; Kenneth Roth; Orville Schell; Sophie C. Silberberg; Gary Sick; Nadine Strossen.

Staff: Aryeh Neier, Executive Director; Kenneth Roth, Deputy Director; Holly J. Burkhalter, Washington Director; Ellen Lutz, California Director; Susan Osnos, Press Director.

## INTERNATIONAL HELSINKI FEDERATION FOR HUMAN RIGHTS

Helsinki Watch is an affiliate of the International Helsinki Federation for Human Rights, a human rights organization that links Helsinki Committees in the following countries of Europe and North America: Austria, Canada, Czechoslovakia, Denmark, England, the Federal Republic of Germany, Finland, France, Hungary, Italy, the Netherlands, Norway, Poland, the Soviet Union, Spain, Sweden, Switzerland, the United States, Yugoslavia.

The Chairman of the International Federation for Human Rights is Karl Johannes von Schwarzenberg; the Secretary General is Gerald Nagler; the Executive Director is Yadja Zeltman.

## Table of Contents

Preface .................................................... i

Introduction .............................................. 1

The Greek Government's Obligations
    Under International Law ........................ 5

    Treaty of Lausanne ............................. 5
    1968 Protocol .................................. 6
    European Convention for the Protection of Human
        Rights and Fundamental Freedoms .......... 6
    Helsinki Final Act ............................. 6
    1989 Concluding Act of Vienna Follow-up Meeting
        to the Conference on Security and Cooperation
        in Europe ............................... 7

The Greek Constitution ................................ 9

Greek Violations of the Human Rights
of the Turkish Minority .............................. 11

    Deprivation of Citizenship ..................... 11
    Freedom of Movement: Passport Seizures ......... 13
    Freedom of Movement in Restricted Areas ........ 14
    Denial of Ethnic Identity ...................... 14
        Cases Against Dr. Sadik Ahmet and
        Mr. Ismail Serif ........................ 17
    Degrading Treatment ............................ 22
    Freedom of Expression .......................... 23
    Religious Freedom .............................. 26
        Mosques ................................. 26
        Selection of Muftis ..................... 28
        Control of the Wakfs (Pious Foundations) .... 29
    Political Freedom .............................. 29

Equal Rights ........................................ 30
    International and National Guarantees ...... 30
    Land and Houses ...................... 32
    Expropriation of Land ................. 35
    Business and Professional Life ........... 36
    Licenses ............................. 37
    Civil Service Jobs .................... 37
    Credit ............................... 39
    Schools .............................. 39
    Schoolbooks ......................... 41

Recommendations .................................. 43
Appendices ....................................... 45

## Acknowledgments

This report is based largely on information gathered by Lois Whitman, Deputy Director of Helsinki Watch, during a fact-finding mission to Western Thrace in May 1990. It was written by Lois Whitman.

## Preface

Between 120,000 and 130,000 ethnic Turks live in Western Thrace, in the northeastern part of Greece. Members of the Turkish minority speak Turkish as well as Greek, send their children to schools in which they are taught in both Turkish and Greek, and are proud of their Turkish origins and resentful of Greek efforts to deny their ethnic identity. The Greek government refers to them as "Greek Moslems," or "Hellenic Moslems," and flatly denies the existence of a Turkish minority in Western Thrace.

Ethnic Turks emphasized to a Helsinki Watch fact-finding mission that went to Western Thrace in May 1990 that they are loyal Greek citizens and that there is no separatist movement in Western Thrace. "We don't want to go to Turkey," a Moslem lawyer said. "We just want the invisible Berlin Wall to come down; we want to have our origins recognized and our human rights protected."

The policy of the Greek government with regard to the Turkish minority seems to be, as described by the Minority Rights Group, a "deliberate policy of discrimination with a long-term aim of assimilation."[1] The findings of the Helsinki Watch mission certainly confirm this analysis. The many abuses of human rights documented in this report reveal a pattern of denying the Turkish minority the rights granted to other Greek citizens; the pattern includes outright deprivation of citizenship; denials of the right to buy land or houses, to set up businesses or to rebuild or repair Turkish schools; restrictions on freedom of expression, movement and religion; and degrading treatment of ethnic Turks by government officials.

The Turkish minority reports that for many years the Greek government has been trying to reduce the number of ethnic Turks in Western Thrace. This has been done by techniques ranging from deprivation of citizenship to "encouraging" emigration to Turkey, to efforts to assimilate the Turkish minority. A Greek policy that began in 1985, for example, made it easier for Greek Turks who are willing to leave Western Thrace to establish themselves in other parts of Greece. It is possible for ethnic Turks to buy land and houses, and to find employment in Athens, on Crete, in Kavala, or in other places in Greece,

---

[1] Minority Rights Group, *Minorities in the Balkans*, Report No. 82, October 1989, page 33.

so long as they are willing to take along their families, to give up residence in Western Thrace and to vote in the new areas. The Turkish minority reported to Helsinki Watch, however, that those who leave cannot get civil service jobs if they identify themselves as Turks or as Moslems, and, of course, that there are no Turkish schools for their children. Sadik Ahmet, a surgeon who is now a member of Parliament, pointed out that "for the rich it's easy to move, but for the poor, impossible."

In any case, the pull of identification with Western Thrace is strong. "This is my fatherland," Dr. Ahmet told Helsinki Watch. "I was born here, I want to stay here. I want to spend my life in Western Thrace. It's the home of my family, my friends, my village, my grandparents. I don't want to leave."

\* \* \*

This is Helsinki Watch's first report on human rights in Greece. Although we have been following for some time the plight of the Turkish minority in Western Thrace, the fact-finding mission on which this report is based was in response to 18-month prison sentences that were handed down to two ethnic Turkish political candidates for Parliament, Dr. Sadik Ahmet and Mr. Ismail Serif, in January 1990, for the crime of using the word "Turkish" to describe the Turkish minority in Western Thrace. The Court held that this act violated the Greek Penal Code by "openly or indirectly inciting citizens to violence or creating rifts among the population at the expense of social peace."

This flagrant denial of the ethnic identity of the Turkish minority in Western Thrace was not an isolated event. The Greek High Court in 1988 had in fact upheld a 1986 decision by the Court of Appeals in Western Thrace in which the Union of Turkish Associations of Western Thrace was ordered closed because it was called "Turkish." The word "Turkish," the court held, could refer only to citizens of Turkey, and its use to describe Greek Moslems was held to endanger public order.

Further research suggested a pattern whereby the Greek government has been denying to the Turkish minority many rights accorded to other Greek citizens, and curtailing their free expression and political freedom. This pattern in a Western democracy like Greece is of great concern to Helsinki Watch. This report describes some of the policies and practices that seriously restrict the human rights of the Turkish minority in Western Thrace.

Greek officials were cooperative and helpful during the Helsinki Watch mission to Western Thrace. The Nomarks (governors) of both Xanthi and Komotini, Constantine Thanopolous and Dionysus Karahalios, gave interviews on short notice. Mr. Evangelos Damianakis, the Greek official responsible for Western Thrace, was extremely generous with his time.

This report could not have been written without the help of the Turkish minority in Western Thrace. Special thanks go to Dr. Sadik Ahmet, Ahmet Faikoglu, Ismail Serif, Ismail Molla Rodoplu, Adem Bekiroglu, Ahmet Haciosman, Ali Muminoglu, Tefikoglu Sabri, Mustafa Arif, Sabri Haci Husseyin, Husseyin Aga and former Mufti Mehmet Emin Aga.

Lois Whitman

New York
August 1990

# Introduction

Turks appear to have settled in Western Thrace in the twelfth century. People of Turkish origin have been living in Western Thrace for hundreds of years. In modern times, Western Thrace has been occupied by Bulgaria (1913-1919) and by the Allied Administration (1919-1920); it has belonged to Greece since 1920.

In 1923 the Lausanne Treaty was signed, putting an end to the Greco-Turkish war. A convention signed at the same time provided for a compulsory exchange of populations:[2] about a million and a quarter Greeks left Turkey for Greece, and about half a million Turks returned to Turkey from Greece.[3] But the convention excluded from the population exchange two groups: Greeks living in Istanbul (then Constantinople) and Turks living in Western Thrace.

Western Thrace is bordered on the north by Bulgaria, on the south by the Aegean Sea, on the east by Turkey, and on the west by the Greek region of Macedonia. It contains three administrative departments or provinces (nomoi): Xanthi, whose capital is the city of Xanthi (Turkish name: Iskece); Rodope, whose capital is Komotini (Gumulcine); and Evros, whose capital is Alexandroupoli (Dedeagac).[4]

Arriving at accurate population figures for the minority groups in Western Thrace is difficult. According to figures submitted to the Lausanne Peace Conference by the Turkish delegation, the population of Western Thrace in 1923 was 191,699, of whom 129,120 (67 percent) were Turks and 33,910 (18 percent) were Greeks; the remaining 28,669 were mostly Bulgarians, along with small numbers of Jews and Armenians. The Turks thus outnumbered the Greeks by about four to

---

[2] See Appendix A for the full text of the Convention, signed at Lausanne, January 30, 1923.

[3] Bernard Lewis, *The Emergence of Modern Turkey*, Second Edition (1968), p. 354.

[4] Since 1977, all Turkish village names have been changed to Greek names; it is forbidden to use Turkish names for official purposes, on pain of fines or imprisonment. In addition, giving the Turkish name in parentheses following the Greek name is not allowed. The Minority Rights Group, *Minorities in the Balkans, op. cit.*, page 33.

one. Greeks claim that the Turkish minority numbered only 103,000 in 1923, which is the number of exemption documents issued by the special Mixed Commission of the League of Nations.[5]

The Turkish delegation also reported that the Turkish minority, mostly farmers, owned 84 percent of the land, and that Bulgarians owned 10 percent and Greeks, largely traders, owned 5 percent. Greek sources dispute these figures as well.

Population and land-ownership figures are quite different today. The population of Western Thrace is now about 360,000; most observers believe that between 120,000 and 130,000 of these (between 33 and 36 percent) are of Turkish origin.[6] In a June 7, 1990, interview published in the Turkish daily newspaper, *Cumhuriyet*, Greek Minister of Justice Athanassios Kanellopoulos said that there are 150,000 Greek citizens of Moslem faith in Western Thrace. This figure includes Turkish Moslems, Pomaks and Gypsies, all of whom are Turkish-speaking. The Greek government contends that these are three separate groups; the Turkish minority claims that all consider themselves Turkish.

The rate of population growth of the Turkish minority is reportedly as high as 2.8 percent. If members of the Turkish minority had not emigrated, its population through natural growth would now be around 500,000, even if it had grown at a rate of only 2 percent. Instead, the current population of 120,000 reflects the fact that between 300,000 and 400,000 Turks have left Western Thrace since 1923. Most of these emigrants have gone to Turkey.[7]

Land ownership, too, has changed dramatically. Instead of owning 84 percent of the land, the Turkish minority now owns between 20 and 40 percent.

The historic enmity between Greece and Turkey has been reflected in Greece's treatment of the Turkish minority. Over the years, ethnic Turks have complained of human rights abuses involving denials

---

[5] Alexis Alexandris, "Political Expediency and Human Rights: Minority Issues between Greece and Turkey," Paper prepared for Minority Rights Conference, March 30-April 1, 1990, Copenhagen, page 5.

[6] The Minority Rights Group, *Minorities in the Balkans, op. cit.*, page 32.

[7] The Greek community in Istanbul, about 100,000 in 1923, is now about 3,500, according to the Greek government.

of civil and political rights, restrictions on freedom of movement and free expression, interference with the free exercise of religion, denial of ethnic identity, degrading treatment, and discrimination on the basis of ethnic origin. Greek authorities deny the existence of the Turkish minority, asserting only that there is a Moslem minority in Greece, a minority population that is homogeneous in religion, but heterogeneous in origin.

## The Greek Government's Obligations Under International Law

The Greek government's obligations to protect and guarantee the rights of the Turkish minority have been established by international treaties and agreements.

### Treaty of Lausanne

Articles 37 through 45 of the Lausanne Treaty of 1923, described as "fundamental laws," set forth the obligations of the Greek and Turkish governments to protect the Turkish and Greek minorities in their territories.[8] Each country agreed to provide:

- o protection of life and liberty without regard to birth, nationality, language, race or religion;

- o free exercise of religion;

- o freedom of movement and of emigration;

- o equality before the law;

- o the same civil and political rights enjoyed by the majority;

- o free use of any language in private, in commerce, in religion, the press and publications, at public meetings and in the courts;

- o the right to establish and control charitable, religious and social institutions and schools;

- o primary schools in which instruction is given in both languages; and

---

[8] See Appendix B for full text of Articles 37 through 45 of the Treaty of Lausanne, signed in Lausanne on July 24, 1923.

o full protection for religious establishments and pious foundations.

## 1968 Protocol

In December 1968, the Greek and Turkish governments signed a protocol issued by a Greek-Turkish cultural commission; among other things, the protocol guaranteed that each country would respect the religious, ethnic and national consciousness of the Greek or Turkish minority within its borders.

## European Convention for the Protection of Human Rights and Fundamental Freedoms

In addition to agreeing to the provisions of the Lausanne treaty that deal directly with the rights of the Turkish minority in Greece, Greece has signed other international documents designed to protect human rights, including the European Convention for Human Rights. That convention establishes broad guarantees for human rights and fundamental freedoms. Among them are the right not be be subjected to inhuman or degrading treatment; the right to a fair trial by an independent, impartial tribunal; the right to freedom of religion, expression, and association; the right to receive information without interference and regardless of frontiers; the right to an effective remedy for violations of human rights; and the right to be free from discrimination because of religion or membership in a national minority.

## Helsinki Final Act

Greece was among the countries in the Conference on Security and Cooperation in Europe (CSCE) that signed the Helsinki Final Act in 1975. Principle VII of that act provides broad guarantees for human rights and fundamental freedoms. It also requires that participating states respect the rights of national minorities within their territories to equality before the law, and to "full opportunity for the actual enjoyment of human rights and fundamental freedoms."

**1989 Concluding Document of the Vienna Follow-Up Meeting to the Conference on Security and Cooperation in Europe (CSCE)**

The 1989 Concluding Document of the Vienna Follow-Up Meeting to the CSCE, which Greece signed, lays out the principles that guide relations between states. Among these are ensuring human rights and fundamental freedoms to everyone within a country's territory without regard to religion or national origin. The document also ensures that no one will be discriminated against for exercising human rights and freedoms. In discussing religious freedom, it sets forth the rights of individuals to organize their own religious structures. It also ensures the rights of national minorities and declares that signatory countries will:

> protect and create conditions for the promotion of the ethnic, cultural, linguistic and religious identity of national minorities on their territory. They will respect the free exercise of rights by persons belonging to such minorities and ensure their full equality with others.

The document states that participating states will respect the right of everyone to leave his own country and to return to it.

## The Greek Constitution

The rights of the Turkish minority in Western Thrace are also protected by the Greek Constitution, enacted in 1975. That document provides that:

o  All Greeks are equal before the law (Art. 4.1);

o  All persons possessing the qualifications for citizenship as specified by law are Greek citizens. Withdrawal of Greek citizenship shall be permitted only in case of voluntary acquisition of another citizenship or of undertaking service contrary to national interests in a foreign country, under the conditions and procedures more specifically provided by law (Art. 4.3);

o  All persons shall have the right to develop freely their personality and to participate in the social, economic and political life of the country, insofar as they do not infringe upon the rights of others or violate the Constitution and moral values (Art. 5.1);

o  All persons living within the Greek territory shall enjoy full protection of their life, honour and freedom, irrespective of nationality, race or language and of religious or political beliefs. Exceptions shall be permitted only in cases provided by international law (Art. 5.2);

o  Individual administrative measures restrictive of the free movement or residence in the country, and of the free exit and entrance therein of every Greek, shall be prohibited (Art. 5.4);

o  The press is free. Censorship and all other preventive measures are prohibited (Art. 14.2).

# Greek Violations of the Human Rights of the Turkish Minority

In spite of the protections set forth in the Treaty of Lausanne, in other international documents to which the government of Greece is a party, and in the Greek Constitution, the Turkish minority in Western Thrace has suffered from significant human rights abuses over the years.[9]

## Deprivation of Citizenship

The Greek Nationality Law, No. 3370, enacted in 1955, states in Chapter B, Section VI, Article 19:

> A person of non-Greek ethnic origin leaving Greece without the intention of returning may be declared as having lost Greek nationality. This also applies to a person of non-Greek ethnic origin born and domiciled abroad. His minor children living abroad may be declared as having lost Greek nationality if both their parents or the surviving parent have lost the same. The Minister of the Interior decides in these matters with the concurring opinion of the National Council.

This law violates two provisions of the Greek Constitution: Article 4.1, which provides that all Greeks are equal before the law, and Article 4.2, which says that "withdrawal of Greek citizenship shall be permitted only in case of voluntary acquisition of another citizenship or of undertaking service contrary to national interests in a foreign country." Article 19 also violates the Concluding Document of the Vienna Follow-up Meeting to the CSCE signed in January 1989, cited earlier, which provides that states will respect the right of everyone to leave his own country and return to it.

Under Article 19, ethnic Turks can be stripped of their citizenship by an administrative decree, without a hearing. According to the U.S. State Department's 1989 Country Report, under Greek law there can be no judicial review and there is no effective right of appeal.

---

[9] The terms "Turkish minority," "Turkish community," "Moslem minority," "Greek Turks" and "ethnic Turks," are used interchangeably in this report. All refer to Greek citizens of Turkish origin in Western Thrace.

The total number of people who have lost their citizenship in this fashion is not clear. According to Nikos Papaconstantinou, the director of the Greek Press and Information Office in New York, Article 19 has not been enforced since the beginning of 1989. However, according to Dr. Sadik Ahmet, a surgeon from Komotini who is now a member of Parliament, there were between 20 and 30 such cases in 1989, and some hundreds over the past years. Others report that the number is in the thousands. Some of the people allegedly deprived of citizenship in 1989 were students who went abroad to study in Turkey or Germany and found when they tried to return that they had lost their citizenship and were not permitted to come back to Greece.

According to lawyers representing the Turkish minority, if an ethnic Turk is out of the country, police ask his or her neighbors if he or she will return to Greece. If the neighbors say no, police send a notice to the Minister of the Interior in Athens, who then decides whether to remove the person's citizenship. A decision to do so is printed in the government newspaper, but the person is not notified.

In one case, Semahat Haliloglu, a soldier, lost his citizenship on July 21, 1989, when he was away in military service.

In 1987, Arap Haliloglu of the village of Lambron lost his Greek nationality. Mr. Haliloglu wrote to the Minister of the Interior and received an answer saying the Ministry would examine his situation, but nothing has happened.

The Minority Rights Group reports on one case that was described in the Athens newspaper, *Rizospastis*, on May 19, 1986. Two "Muslim origin Greek citizens" from a village near Komotini were refused re-entry and deported after visiting their son who was studying in Istanbul.[10]

To regain one's citizenship after it has been removed is almost impossible. An ethnic Turkish lawyer told Helsinki Watch that he knew of only one such case: the case of journalist Sabahattin Galip. And, in that case, after the highest court ordered Mr. Galip's citizenship restored a few years ago, the Minister of the Interior brought an action against him under Article 20 of the Nationality Law, saying that Mr. Galip had taken action against Greece outside of Greece, and Mr. Galip again lost

---

[10] The Minority Rights Group, *Minorities in the Balkans, op. cit.*, page 33.

his citizenship. This act was based on Mr. Galip's friendship with Turks in Istanbul who had formed an association in Istanbul to help Turks who move from Western Thrace to Istanbul.

In 1989, Mayor Ihtiyar Fikri of Ehinos complained to the Minister of the Interior, the Prime Minister and others, saying that people of Turkish origin were losing their Greek citizenship for no reason. As a result, the Nomark of Xanthi province (a governor appointed by the Ministry of the Interior) called the mayor to the police station and asked him why he had written such things. The Nomark then brought a case against him for his complaints; that case is now in the courts.

The threat of stripping citizenship from ethnic Turks who leave the country temporarily clearly affects their freedom of movement. A number of ethnic Turks told Helsinki Watch they were afraid to leave the country, fearing that their citizenship might be taken away.

**Freedom of Movement; Passport Seizures**

The Greek government also inhibits Turkish Greeks' freedom of movement by seizing their passports. The Turkish community reports that many passports were seized in 1989; in some cases, police came to people's homes and demanded their passports; in others, people returning to Greece were told that their passports were no longer valid, and the passports were confiscated. In most cases, the passports were returned between two and eight months later, with no explanation. According to the Turkish community, passports of between forty and fifty people were confiscated in this way during 1989; most got them back within a few months, but in four or five cases, the passports were not returned for ten months.

One of the seized passports belonged to lawyer Adem Bekiroglu; it was taken for three months in 1989, as he was on his way to Turkey. When Mr. Bekiroglu asked why it was being confiscated, the officer said, "I don't know the reason; I have my orders." Mr. Bekiroglu filed a court action; three months later he was called on the phone and told to "come and get your passport." He picked up the document at the police station; he was never given a reason for its confiscation.

In another case, the passport of Mustafa Havus, an independent candidate for Parliament, was confiscated 10 days before an election in 1989. In yet another, the passport of Ahmet Haciosman, an imam in Komotini, was taken on January 10, 1990, and returned on May 4, 1990.

Mr. Haciosman was called to the police station to pick up his passport; there, he reported, a policeman told him, "You are very fanatic; you should be more careful to be a good citizen." Mr. Haciosman said that he replied, "If I've done anything illegal, why don't you take me to court?"

The confiscation of passports for no reason, without a hearing and without an opportunity for judicial review, violates the Greek Constitution and international agreements on freedom of movement, and constitutes harassment of the Turkish community and a denial of its right to travel.

### Freedom of Movement in Restricted Areas

Much of Western Thrace is a restricted military area; one must have official permission to enter. This very large area of land borders on Bulgaria. According to leaders of the Turkish minority, about 25,000 ethnic Turks (largely Pomaks) live in the Xanthi portion of the restricted area, and 10,000 in the Komotini portion; five to seven Turkish villages are located in the Evros portion. Inhabitants of the military area are severely restricted in their movements. The area is completely closed between midnight and 5:00 A.M., and at all times, according to the Minority Rights Group, inhabitants are restricted to an area within 30 kilometers of their villages.[11] They are quite isolated from the rest of Western Thrace, and, according to members of the Turkish minority, their schools are inferior and do not prepare the children for work other than farming.

### Denial of Ethnic Identity

The Greek government denies the existence of a Turkish minority within its borders; government spokesmen say there are no Turks in Western Thrace. Mr. Constantine Thanopolous, the Nomark of Xanthi, told Helsinki Watch, "There is no Turkish minority in Western Thrace. The Lausanne Treaty speaks only of 'the Moslems of Greece.'" Prime Minister Constantine Mitsotakis, responding to a journalist's question in Washington, D.C., on June 18, 1990, said, "There are no Greek Turks. There are Greek Moslems in Western Thrace. This is

---

[11] Minority Rights Group, *Minorities in the Balkans, op. cit.*, page 32.

what was foreseen by the Lausanne Treaty."[12] As these examples indicate, the government refers to the ethnic Turks as "Greek Moslems," or "Hellenic Moslems," or "the Moslem minority." It views the Turks as a religious minority, rather than as an ethnic or a national minority.

The Turkish community vigorously rejects this interpretation. "There are many nations that have the Moslem religion," Mustafa Arif, the former head of the Turkish Youth Association, told Helsinki Watch. "If you call us 'the Moslem minority' you can't tell our origin. There is a difference between one's origin and one's religion. When they won't let us call ourselves 'Turks,' they are denying our origin. We are loyal Greek citizens, but we are Turks, and we want the right to call ourselves Turks."

The Greek government's practices and policies regarding the Turkish minority's "right to call themselves Turkish" have changed over the years. The Turkish community has gathered a number of documents showing the use of the word "Turkish" in official documents in the past:

o photographs of Turkish elementary schools showing:

a Turkish school in the village of Kalhandos in Komotini about 30 years ago, in which a sign identifies the school as a Turkish elementary school, and in which the name appears written in both Greek and Turkish;

a Turkish school in the village of Makre in Evros taken about twenty years ago, in which the school is called a Turkish school, but the name is written only in Greek; the Turkish Central elementary school of Xanthi, taken in 1967, in which the name is written only in Greek;

in contrast, a current Turkish elementary school, in which the name "Turkish" does not appear in either Turkish or Greek;

o A geography book dated 1933, written in Turkish, and described as a "Turkish book;"

---

[12] *The Turkish Times*, July 1, 1990.

- protocols for the program in Turkish elementary schools for the school year, 1957-1958, in which the schools are referred to as "Turkish schools;"

- an elementary school diploma dated June 10, 1957, written in both Greek and Turkish, in which Hatice Iman, 13 years old, is identified as a "Turk;"

- two emergency orders dated 1954 and 1955 in which the chief administrator of Thrace orders municipalities to change all signs from "Moslem minority" to "Turkish minority" (see Appendix C).

- a letter dated October 10, 1985, from the president of the Greek Parliament, stating the term "Greek Moslems" must be used, as the minority's origins are Greek, not Turkish;

- a July 1989 letter written by Dr. Sadik Ahmet, then a member of Parliament, to the president of Greece, referring to the "Turkish Moslem minority;" the letter was returned by the president, who told Dr. Ahmet the letter was unacceptable because of the term, "Turkish Moslem minority," but would be accepted if Dr. Ahmet used the phrase, "Moslem minority."

Greek courts have actually outlawed the use of the word "Turkish" to describe the Turkish minority. In 1988, the Greek High Court affirmed a 1986 decision by the Court of Appeals of Thrace in which the Union of Turkish Associations of Western Thrace was ordered closed. The Court held that the word "Turkish" referred to citizens of Turkey, and could not be used to describe citizens of Greece; the use of the word "Turkish" to describe Greek Moslems was held to endanger public order.[13]

---

[13] In spite of this decree, the word "Turkish" is still sometimes used in relation to the Turkish minority. For example, a 1988 order from the President of the Arios Pagos, the Greek High Court, in File Number 473, refers to Dr. Sadik Ahmet as a "Turkish doctor" from the "Turkish minority."

When word reached the Turkish minority of the High Court's decision, about 10,000 people demonstrated against it in Western Thrace. According to members of the Turkish minority, it was the first time ethnic Turks had taken to the streets. Police broke up the demonstration with force, and many demonstrators were beaten and injured. Twenty were taken to the hospital; three were seriously injured.

Later, some of those injured in the incident were charged with beating police. On April 30, 1990, a court in Patras found six men guilty and sentenced them to 40 days in prison. The names of four of these men are Mustafa Bosnak, Necmi Salih, Yakup Mehmet, and Niyazi Topol. At present they are out of prison, appealing the sentences.

As a result of the High Court's decision, most Turkish associations have remained closed. Mustafa Arif, the president of the Turkish Youth Association, told Helsinki Watch that his group no longer exists officially. Police took down the sign that said "Turkish Youth Association," and told Mr. Arif that he would be permitted to call his group the "Moslem Youth Association." As a matter of principle, the group refused to change its name.

According to Mr. Arif, the government's attitude toward the use of the word "Turkish" dates back to the period of military government in the 1970s. First, officials took down signs that said "Turkish." Then the Nomark of Komotini brought a court proceeding to outlaw the use of the word "Turkish" in associations; a court concurred, but that decision was not enforced. The situation worsened after the Turkish action in Cyprus in 1974; at that time the Greek government expressed concern that Turkey would attempt to invade Western Thrace and certain Greek islands.

**The Cases Against Dr. Sadik Ahmet and Mr. Ismail Serif**: Perhaps the most egregious Greek action denying the ethnic identity of the Turkish minority occurred when court cases were brought against Dr. Sadik Ahmet and Mr. Ismail Serif in January 1990.

Dr. Ahmet was elected a member of Parliament in the election of June 1989. Shortly thereafter, a second election was called, to be held on November 5, 1989. In October 1989, Dr. Ahmet and Mr. Serif, independent candidates for Parliament in the election to be held in November, distributed campaign literature that referred by name to the

Turkish minority. Following the election,[14] both men received subpoenas for a trial to be held on January 25, 1990. They were charged with:

- slander and misinformation in Komotini during the last ten days of October 1989, in violation of Articles 245, 320 and 321 of the Criminal Procedure Law, by saying that candidates of the New Democracy, Left Coalition, and PASOK parties had created an atmosphere of terror and anarchy; and

- violating Article 192 of the Penal Code by "openly or indirectly inciting citizens to violence or creating rifts among the population at the expense of social peace" by the use of the word "Turkish."

At the conclusion of the two-day trial in Komotini on January 26, 1990, both men were found innocent of slander and misinformation, but guilty of disturbing public order under Penal Code Article 192. Each was sentenced to 18 months in prison and immediately led away to start serving his sentence. Leaving the courtroom, Dr. Ahmet declared, "I am being taken to prison just because I am a Turk. If being a Turk is a crime, I repeat here that I am a Turk and I will remain so. My message to the minority in Western Thrace is that they should not forget they are Turks."[15]

The trial did not comply with the European Human Rights Convention's requirement of "a fair trial by an independent, impartial tribunal." Turgut Kazan, the President of the Istanbul Bar Association, observed the trial, along with other international observers. Kazan reported:

---

[14] Neither man was elected in November 1989. Dr. Ahmet's candidacy was invalidated on technical grounds.

[15] *Dateline*, February 3, 1990.

The trial started on January 25, with demonstrations; a crowd which had filled the courtroom applauded the judges and the prosecutor, as if they were going to battle, from which they expected "victory". . .

Throughout the proceedings, two of the three judges and the prosecutor shouted at the defendants with open malice. Particularly, the second judge frequently jumped to his feet in order to increase the effect of his shouting.

The crowd which filled the courtroom cheered the prosecutor and the judges and cursed the defendants with such noise that the words of the defendants and their lawyers could not be heard.

The presiding judge viewed this turmoil calmly, with a smile on his face.

When the defendants told the court that they were of Turkish origin, the judges shouted back, "Then why don't you go to Turkey?"

Witnesses were led by the judges and when their testimony did not please the judges, they were abused. The witnesses who pleased the court were allowed to testify for 30-40 minutes. But those who testified in favor of the defense were quickly dismissed.

Article 192 under which the defendants were tried covered offenses which "directed the citizens to disrupt public order by openly encouraging the use of force." But none of the witnesses testifed to the existence of the use of force or encouragement in that direction.

When the defense lawyers left the court as a protest at the hostile behavior of the second judge, the defendants requested a recess to appoint new lawyers. The court denied this basic right.

Defendant Ibrahim Serif's court-appointed interpreter did not know Turkish. But the court continued the proceedings regardless of this fundamental defect.

The prosecutor shouted at Dr. Sadik Ahmet: "Your end will be like Ceausescu's."

In other words, this was not a court of law, but a political demonstration. The proceedings were filmed by the Dutch TV, and viewing of this film will confirm our observations.

In the end, the verdict was announced. The defendants were sentenced to 18 months in prison and their civil rights were revoked. They were arrested there and sent to prison.

The spectators shouted victory slogans and the demonstration which had started in the court continued in the streets; Mrs. Sadik Ahmet, the Dutch TV crew and our delegation were attacked by the mob.

In response to a letter of protest sent to then-Prime Minister Xefonon Zolotas by Helsinki Watch, Stefanos Stathatos, the director of the Diplomatic Office of the Prime Minister, wrote that "the trial was held in strict observance of the Greek penal procedures . . . . [T]he Judiciary is completely independent in applying legislation to all Greek citizens without exception."

According to information provided to Helsinki Watch in August 1990 by Nikos Papaconstantinou, the director of the Greek Press and Information Office in New York:

> Messrs. A. Sadik and I. Serif were not charged because they used the adjective "Turkish." They were charged because of the way they used it, trying to create political destabilization, national, racial and religious contest, which, if allowed to continue, would result in creating some sort of a separatist movement in Western Thrace. It should be underlined that they were charged for the consequences of the use of the adjective and not for its use *per se*.

Two days after the trial, violence erupted in Komotini. Mobs of Greeks ran through the streets, beating ethnic Turks and smashing windows of Turkish shops and offices. Twenty-one people were injured and over 400 businesses belonging to Turkish Greeks were damaged. An eye-witness told Helsinki Watch that he had seen a mob of between 40 and 50 running wild, smashing windows, hitting people and vandalizing cars; he watched a police car drive slowly behind the mob, making no effort to stop the rampage. Foreign observers reported that Greek shops were untouched, and that police did not attempt to halt the destruction.

Ismail Molla Rodoplu, a journalist in Komotini who has served one term in Parliament, told Helsinki Watch that between 50 and 60 people had smashed all the windows in his office, broken down the door, and run through his office, hitting Aga Mehmet Muftiya with a piece of iron as they ran through.

Members of the Turkish minority told Helsinki Watch in May 1990 that a total of about 1,000 people had taken part in the violence, but that the core appeared to consist of about 150 extremists. The government has said that it would reimburse shopkeepers and others for their losses, but nothing has happened. The ethnic Turks estimate the damage at about half a million dollars; they have many photographs showing broken windows and empty, looted stores.

Following the violence, the Turkish consul in Komotini, Kemal Gur, was declared *persona non grata* and expelled from Greece for referring to the Turkish minority as "our kinsmen." The Turkish government retaliated by expelling the Greek consul in Istanbul, Mr. Ilias Klis.

Dr. Ahmet and Mr. Serif spent 64 days in prison in Thessaloniki.[16] An appeals court then affirmed their convictions, but released them from prison and ordered them to pay fines (about $2800 for Ahmet; about $1875 for Serif) in place of the remainder of their prison terms.

Because he had been released, Dr. Ahmet was permitted to run for Parliament; he was elected an independent member of Parliament on April 8, 1990.[17]

---

[16] Dr. Sadik told Helsinki Watch that he was treated correctly in prison, largely, he believed, because of a visit by Eric Siesby, the chairman of the Danish Helsinki Committee. After Professor Siesby's visit, two of the seven inmates in Dr. Ahmet's crowded cell were removed, and the guards addressed him more politely, offering to help him if they could.

[17] Another member of the Turkish community, Ahmet Faikoglu, was elected at the same time as an independent to represent Xanthi; he had earlier served as a member of Parliament in the PASOK party.

Two other cases were filed against Ahmet and Serif for campaign literature referring to the "Turkish minority."[18] The trials, originally scheduled for February 8 and 15, 1990, were postponed after international protests against the January decision and have not been held.

These three cases were not the first against Sadik Ahmet; on June 25, 1988, he was sentenced to two and a half years in prison on charges of violating Penal Code Article 192 by collecting "false signatures" from the Moslem minority in Western Thrace on a petition alleging human rights breaches by the Greek government, including a policy of assimilation and forced emigration of the Turkish minority. Dr. Ahmet told Helsinki Watch that he had collected 15,000 signatures in six months in 1986 by going from village to village, talking with people in coffee houses. In the court case, he was also accused of spreading false information about Greece by claiming that the authorities do not permit purchase of real estate by members of the Turkish minority. In December 1989, an appeals court in Thessaloniki postponed a ruling on Dr. Ahmet's appeal. He has not served any time in prison because of this conviction.

**Degrading Treatment**

The European Convention for the Protection of Human Rights and Fundamental Freedoms provides that individuals cannot be subjected to inhuman or degrading treatment. In spite of that guarantee, the Turkish minority in Western Thrace continues to experience degrading treatment in the form of continued harassment by police:

> o   Greek security forces frequently call in for interrogation members of the Turkish minority who have helped outside observers. After the February 1990 visit to Western Thrace of Professor Eric Siesby of the Danish Helsinki Committee, for example, lawyer Adem

---

[18] See Appendix D for a copy of Dr. Ahmet's subpoena for the February 8 trial; the February 15 subpoena is substantially the same.

Bekiroglu was called to the police station and asked why he had helped Professor Siesby and his party; specifically, why he had taken Prof. Siesby to the home of the director of the Moslem religious school.

o  Ethnic Turks are often threatened by police. When imam Ahmet Haciosman called the police to complain about being followed in May, for example, he was told, "You ought to be beaten again so that you would understand," a reference to the beatings of ethnic Turks during the rioting following the convictions of Sadik Ahmet and Ismail Serif.

o  Lawyers who represent the Turkish minority are sometimes harassed by police. Adem Bekiroglu told Helsinki Watch that seven police officers had come to his office in 1983 and spent eight hours searching everything, including his confidential legal papers.

o  The head of the Security Police, Atanasios Dalamangidis, orders police surveillance of many Moslem Turks; Dr. Sadik Ahmet reports that his home is watched continually. Although he has complained, nothing has happened.

o  Outside observers investigating the situation of the Turkish minority are also targeted by security forces. A German lawyer, Hans Heldmann, for example, who attended the trial of Dr. Sadik Ahmet and Mr. Ismail Serif, was beaten by police; he has filed a complaint against Greece at the European Commission of Human Rights. The May Helsinki Watch mission was openly followed throughout the Komotini area, and sporadically followed in Xanthi.

**Freedom of Expression**

The right to freedom of expression is guaranteed in the European Convention for the Protection of Human Rights and Fundamental Freedoms; that convention also protects the right to receive information without interference and regardless of frontiers.

Article 14 of the Greek Constitution states:

> 1. Every person may express and propagate his thoughts orally, in writing and through the press in compliance with the laws of the State.
>
> 2. The press is free. Censorship and all other preventive measures are prohibited.[19]

In spite of these national and international protections, the free expression rights of the Turkish minority in Western Thrace are frequently violated. On the positive side, the Turkish minority is allowed to issue newspapers and magazines in the Turkish language; newspapers and magazines published in Turkey, however, are not allowed entry into Western Thrace, nor are Turkish books. In addition, Turkish television and sometimes Turkish radio are jammed.

Five small Turkish-language newspapers, consisting of a few sheets each, are published weekly in Komotini and Xanthi, along with two small monthly magazines.[20] The oldest newspaper, *Akin*, has been

---

[19] Article 14.3 of the Constitution does provide for the seizure of newspapers or other publications in case of:
    a) an offense against the Christian or any other known religion;
    b) an insult against the person of the President of the Republic;
    c) a publication which discloses information on the composition, equipment and set-up of the armed forces or the fortifications of the country, or which aims at the violent overthrow of the regime or is directed against the territorial integrity of the State;
    d) an obscene article obviously offensive to public decency, in the cases stipulated by law.

[20] According to Greek Information Office Director Papaconstantinou, sixteen newspapers and magazines are currently published in the Turkish language in Western Thrace.

published in Komotini for 40 years. The weekly, *Yanki (Echo)*, which has been published since 1987, had difficulty starting up. In order to publish a newspaper, one needs permission from the Nomark (the chief administrator of the province). According to the Turkish minority, the Nomark refused such permission until Ahmet Faikoglu became a member of Parliament, representing Xanthi; he was then able to obtain permission from the Nomark. Mr. Faikoglu now issues a small weekly newspaper called *Ogut (Advice)*.

Journalists told Helsinki Watch that newspapers cannot print editorials criticizing the Greek government. A number of journals have been taken to court for articles they have printed. *Gercek (Truth)*, a paper published in Komotini by Ismail Molla Rodoplu, a former member of Parliament, has been taken to court three times since 1978. The three cases concerned an article on the pressures against the Turkish community; an article on whether the residents of Ehinos, in the restricted military area along the border with Bulgaria, are Pomaks or Turks; and one on the government's expropriation of land from Turks for a university. Mr. Rodoplu was found innocent in each case. *Gercek* was also forced to pay a large fine--four and a half million drachmas (about $28,000) -- for what Mr. Rodoplu described as "technical violations." He believes that the fine was assessed for political reasons.

Dr. Sadik Ahmet has published 15 issues of a weekly newspaper called *Guven (Trust)* in Komotini. Dr. Ahmet has been taken to court twice in 1990 for articles published in the journal: one criticized the foreign minister and one discussed the illegal seizure of passports from the Turkish minority. Both cases are pending.

When asked why these legal actions had been taken against the Turkish-language local press, Mr. Evangelos Damianakis, the Director of Political Affairs for Thrace, told Helsinki Watch that those newspapers were spreading lies about the state.

Turkish-language newspapers published in Turkey are not permitted to come into the country. When asked the reason for this ban, Mr. Damianakis said that no one wanted to distribute them, and that, anyway, one could drive for three hours to buy one across the border in Turkey.

When told of Mr. Damianakis's statement, members of the Turkish minority laughed, and two different political figures said they themselves were eager to import and distribute Turkish newspapers from Turkey.

Helsinki Watch was told by many members of the Turkish minority that television programs from Turkey have been jammed since June 1989; before that, it was possible to watch Turkish television on the second channel. Member of Parliament Ahmet Faikoglu told Helsinki Watch that in some villages it is possible to see television broadcasts from Turkey: two of the villages are in Komotini, and the others are outside of Alexandroupoli. But while it is possible to receive by satellite 20 channels in Western Thrace -- many Greek channels as well as channels from Germany, Britain, France, Luxembourg, the United States -- it is impossible for most people to receive television transmitted from Turkey.

The Turkish minority reports that Turkish radio broadcasts have also been jammed by local Greek radio stations in some areas; villagers in Mavromati village outside of Komotini, however, told Helsinki Watch that they were able to receive radio broadcasts from Turkey.

Political Affairs Director, Evangelos Damianakis, denied to Helsinki Watch that Turkish television and radio were jammed.

Mr. Damianakis also flatly denied that Turkish-language books are not permitted to be brought in from Turkey, and offered to show the Helsinki Watch mission bookstores with Turkish books. However, in four of the approximately six bookstores in Xanthi, Helsinki Watch found only one Turkish-language book, a children's book entitled *Paul of Tarsus*. Although these bookstores had many books from Germany, England, France, Italy and the United States, they had no books from Turkey, other than the copy of *Paul of Tarsus*.

Bookstores and newsstands in Komotini and Xanthi had many magazines and newspapers from many countries in Western Europe, as well as the United States, but none from Turkey.

**Religious Freedom**

The Turkish minority in Western Thrace has complained about restrictions by the Greek government on its religious freedom. According to the Lausanne Treaty, the Turkish minority is entitled to freedom of religion and to the right to control charitable and religious institutions. In addition, the January 1989 Concluding Document of the Vienna Follow-up Meeting to the CSCE sets forth the rights of individuals to organize their own religious structures.

The Turkish community believes that these international law guarantees have been violated by the Greek government in three ways: by denying permission to repair or rebuild old mosques or to build new ones, by denying the right to choose the muftis, who are the chief religious officers, and by efforts to control the Turkish minority's wakfs (charitable foundations).

**Mosques**: Citizens of Western Thrace are required to secure permits to buy or sell property, to repair houses, and to build or repair mosques. According to ethnic Turks, permission has not been granted to repair many aging mosques that are in urgent need of repair. Members of the Turkish community showed the Helsinki Watch mission such mosques in villages surrounding both Komotini and Xanthi:

- In Iasmos Helsinki Watch photographed a half-built minaret which the community has been trying for 25 years to get permission to complete.

- In the village of Ziloti, outside of Xanthi, Helsinki Watch saw a small mosque; according to villager Salih Ramadan, the Imam of Ziloti had been applying to the Nomark to enlarge the mosque since 1985. He had applied first to Stellos Vafiadis, an official of the municipality, and then to the Nomark. The village had received permission only to repair a hole in the roof.

- In Diomilia village, outside of Xanthi, Helsinki Watch saw an old mosque in disrepair; member of Parliament Ahmet Faikoglu told Helsinki Watch that the community had been seeking permission to repair it for 15 years.

- In Komotini Helsinki Watch saw the remains of a 600-year-old mosque that was demolished by the government in late 1989; the government has declared its intention to rebuild the mosque, but as yet no steps have been taken to do so.

- The Turkish community provided Helsinki Watch with a copy of a letter dated February 4, 1985, in which the Nomark of Komotini wrote that permission from the Greek Archbishop was required in order to build a mosque (see Appendix E).

Lawyer Adem Bekiroglu told Helsinki Watch that, although no licenses to build new mosques have been granted for many years, it is sometimes possible during election campaigns to obtain licenses to repair old ones. The Nomark of Xanthi, Constantine Thanopolous, told Helsinki Watch that seven or eight permits to repair old mosques had been approved in the last ten months. Political director Damianakis showed Helsinki Watch a photograph of a mosque that he said was being repaired in Komotini.

**Selection of Muftis**: There are three muftis (religious heads of the Moslem communities) in Western Thrace: in Xanthi, Komotini and Evros. The Lausanne Treaty provides not only for free exercise of religion by the Turkish minority, but also for the right to establish and control religious institutions. In addition, Greek law Number 2345 of 1920 states that muftis must be elected by the Moslem people. According to the Turkish community, this law has never been enforced; instead, muftis have been appointed by the Greek government. According to Nikos Papaconstantinou, Director of the Greek Press and Information Office in New York, muftis are appointed by the Minister of Religious Affairs following a proposal submitted by a committee of Moslem religious leaders.

Mufti Mehmet Emin Aga of Xanthi, who was appointed by the Nomark of Xanthi in February 1990, told Helsinki Watch in May that the government had interfered with the religious practices and beliefs of the Turkish minority by not allowing them to choose their spiritual leaders. As an example, he pointed to the recent appointment of Hafiz Cemali as mufti of Komotini. The day after our interview, Mufti Aga resigned, stating that he had accepted the job on condition that the Greek government activate law number 2345, which calls for the election of Moslem religious leaders by members of the community. Mufti Aga stated that by appointing Cemali as mufti of Komotini, the Greek authorities had shown that they have no intention of reactivating the 1920 law.[20]

The issue of the selection of muftis is of great concern to the Turkish community. While the Helsinki mission was in Western Thrace, leaders of the Turkish minority held several meetings, trying to decide how best to handle the situation. Member of Parliament Ahmet Faikoglu

---

[20] *Dateline*, May 19, 1990.

met with imams in Komotini after Mufti Aga's resignation, and announced that the community would launch protest demonstrations if the Greek authorities chose a successor to Mufti Aga instead of allowing the Turkish community to choose one. The selection of muftis was one of the first issues taken up with Prime Minister Constantine Mitsotakis by Dr. Sadik Ahmet on May 14, 1990, in his first meeting with the prime minister after the April elections. Dr. Ahmet asked the prime minister to make changes in the present practices to permit the Moslem minority to elect its religious leaders.

**Control of the Wakfs (Pious Foundations):** The Turkish community has also been angered by Greek efforts to control their wakfs, which are religious endowments or charitable trusts. According to the Moslem community, the directors of the wakfs were elected by the community before the military junta came to power in 1967. Then, in 1980, law No. 1091 was passed, which, among other things, called for the administration of the wakfs by a board of five administrators selected by the Nomark, who was also given the power to approve the wakfs' budgets. This law was deeply resented by the Turkish minority; it has not yet been enforced. Ethnic Turks believe that this law violates their rights under Greek law, the Greek Constitution and the Lausanne treaty, in the provisions cited earlier.

### Political Freedom

All Greek citizens, including ethnic Turks, have the right to vote in national and local elections. However, during the two parliamentary elections held in 1989, in June and in November, the Turkish minority alleged a number of violations of its political rights. The violations claimed in connection with the November 1989 elections included:

- o  Turkish-Greek border crossings were closed shortly before elections to keep ethnic Turks from returning to Greece to vote;

- o  Air connections between Athens and Western Thrace were blocked during the week of November 5, 1989;

- o  Bus service to Western Thrace was cancelled the day before elections;

- The applications of Dr. Sadik Ahmet and Ismail Serif to run for Parliament were rejected just before election day;

- Greek authorities bussed in thousands of soldiers to vote in Western Thrace, in an attempt to outweigh the ethnic Turks' votes;

- There were 231 ballot boxes in Turkish districts for the June 15, 1989, elections, but only 190 for the November elections, forcing some ethnic Turks to travel between one and two hours to vote;

- Counting of 44 ballot boxes in Xanthi and Komotini was halted between 11:00 p.m. on November 5 and 2:00 a.m. November 6. Vote totals were not released;

- Ethnic Turks were not allowed to vote until late in the afternoon, after government officials and servicemen;

- Some ethnic Turks were beaten at the polls;

- Fifty polling places in Turkish districts were closed before the announced closing time, despite long lines of people waiting to vote; they were reopened only following protests by opposition parties;

- No votes at all for Turkish candidates were listed in the village of Sofular, a Turkish stronghold.

Members of the Turkish minority told Helsinki Watch in May 1990, however, that the April 1990 Parliamentary elections had been relatively free of violations of the Turkish community's right to vote. They attributed this change to the presence of outside observers, including Professor Eric Siesby, the head of the Danish Helsinki Committee, and Bjorn Cato Funnemark, the General Secretary of the Norwegian Helsinki Committee.

**Equal Rights**

**International and National Guarantees**: The Turkish minority in Greece has been guaranteed equal rights by both international agreements and the Greek Constitution.

Article 39 of the Lausanne Treaty of 1923 states:

> All the inhabitants of Turkey, without distinction of religion, shall be equal before the law.

Article 45 of that treaty says:

> The rights conferred by the provisions of the present Section on the non-Moslem minorities of Turkey will be similarly conferred by Greece on the Moslem minority in her territory.

Article 4.1 of the Greek Constitution states that all Greeks are equal before the law.
Article 5.1 says:

> All persons shall have the right to develop freely their personality and to participate in the social, economic and political life of the country, insofar as they do not infringe upon the rights of others or violate the Constitution and moral values.

In spite of these protections, the Turkish minority in Western Thrace told Helsinki Watch that it has frequently been denied rights routinely accorded to non-Moslem Greeks. The Greek government, on the other hand, denies that the Turkish minority is treated differently from other Greek citizens.

Perhaps the major human rights concern expressed to Helsinki Watch by the Turkish community in May 1990 was its inability to buy or sell land, to buy, sell, build or repair houses, to build or repair its schools, to build, enlarge or repair mosques--activities that it claims are permitted to other Greek citizens in Western Thrace. The Turkish minority reports that the same denials take place in the commercial area; that ethnic Turks are not given permission to buy or build businesses, to practice their professional skills, to acquire necessary machinery for businesses and the like. In addition, ethnic Turks told Helsinki Watch that it is extremely difficult to get licenses to drive tractors, a major concern of the farmers in the area, who make up most of the ethnic Turkish population. The Turkish minority reports that it has also been difficult for Turks to obtain ordinary drivers' licenses.

**Land and Houses**:  Dr. Sadik Ahmet told Helsinki Watch that everyone must get permission from the Nomarks to buy or sell land, houses or businesses. According to lawyer Adem Bekiroglu, Law No. 1366, passed in 1938, provides that all Greeks need licenses to buy or rent any land. A measure originally enacted to control Communists, it is now used against the Turkish minority, according to Mr. Bekiroglu.  "A lot of people in the Turkish community have the money to buy or build houses, but they can't get licenses. If a Greek Christian wants to buy land, he can get a license the same day, but a Moslem Turk will get no answer. He will be told to return in a month; then the application is lost; then the Nomark's office will not give him the file number. Without the file number, he cannot demand help from the courts. The only legal remedy is to go to the High Court in Athens, and that procedure is very expensive--it costs as much as buying the land. So no one does it. And as for selling land, a Turk can't even sell his own house to a relative without getting permission, and the permission is usually not given. And you can't even repair your own ceiling without getting a special permit. If you do it without permission and the authorities find out, you may be assessed a huge fine."

Sadik Ahmet lives in a modest flat in Komotini, but can afford and wants very much to build a house for his family. "As a member of Parliament, I cannot be denied permission to build a house now," Dr. Ahmet said. "But this is something that I want for all of our people, not just for myself."

Mr. Constantine Thanopolous, the Nomark of Xanthi, flatly denied to Helsinki Watch that the Turkish community (which he referred to as the "Moslem minority") could not buy houses or land. He said that more than 100 contracts for Moslem families to buy land and houses in Xanthi had been approved by his office during the nine months he has served as Nomark. He said that more than 30 percent of Moslems have new buildings which they have built during the last 14 years.

According to Nomark Thanopolous, Law No. 1316 sets limitations on the sale of land; everyone who wants to sell land must submit an application. "Every day my committee signs licenses for the sale of land," he said.

As to repairs of houses, Mr. Thanopolous said at first that no applications to buy, build or repair houses were pending; later, after his secretary brought him some documents, he said that ten applications were pending for house repairs. In those cases, he said, the applications were lacking some documents. "Our service immediately gives licenses to repair houses," he said. "This is a regular procedure for all citizens."

Members of the Turkish minority drove the Helsinki Watch mission to various sections of Xanthi and Komotini, and to small villages surrounding both cities. The differences between the Turkish and non-Turkish areas were striking; whether one is in a Turkish or non-Turkish area is readily apparent. In the Turkish areas, houses were small, simple one-story buildings, frequently needing repair. In the Greek Christian areas, the houses were usually well-cared-for two-story buildings. Roads, schools and playgrounds were significantly better in non-Turkish areas. According to Dr. Sadik Ahmet, Turkish villages cannot get permission to build new roads or repair old ones. If they take such actions without permission, they are subjected to very large penalties. Imam Ahmet Haciosman says that roads are generally not paved in Turkish villages, and water and electricity are often not supplied.

In the Turkish village of Kalamokastro, outside of Komotini, there were many dirt roads and small one-story houses. In the next village, Siderohori, a Greek Christian village, there were paved roads, as well as two-story houses, and a pleasant school with a nice playground. In the Rembi section of Xanthi, Parliamentarian Ahmet Faikoglu showed Helsinki Watch an area with small, one-story Turkish houses, nestled among larger, well-cared-for Greek houses.

Asked the reason for the differences between Greek Christian and Moslem Turkish villages, Nomark Thanopolous said that the differences existed only in the flat areas; that Moslems in the mountain areas (the restricted military zone) had big, beautiful houses. These, he said, were lived in by Pomaks. "In the flat areas," he said, "the Moslems have poorer homes than the Christians because the Moslems prefer to invest their money in Turkey. The usual practice of Moslems is to take their money to Turkey and invest in blocks of flats there. With the high inflation rate in Turkey, it's sixteen times more profitable to invest it there, rather than in Greece."

When asked the same question, Nomark Dionysus Karahalios of Komotini told Helsinki Watch that the houses of the Moslem minority were poorer because that was the manner in which the Moslems preferred to live. "It is not a prohibition on the part of the administration," he said. "You have seen the way the women dress; the men want their women to dress in the Islamic manner, and that's the way they like to live."

Evangelos Damianakis, the Greek official in charge of Western Thrace, told Helsinki Watch that it was not correct that the Moslem minority were not given permission to build houses. He said that the houses of the Greek Christian and Moslem communities were different because of social and economic factors. "Their religion keeps them from being assimilated," he said, "and it keeps them retarded, and away from civilization. If they are not happy in Greece, they can go back to Turkey. Most of the farmers have a good income and a higher standard of living than they would in Turkey. There are no substantial reasons for their grievances. Minorities are always unhappy, but the Moslems in Western Thrace have no substantive grievances."

The Turkish minority says that because of the difficulty of getting permits to build houses, some ethnic Turks have built houses illegally; these houses have no water and no electricity. If illegal houses are discovered by the authorities, the owners are required to pay fines as large as the cost of constructing the house. But, according to the Turkish community, if Greek Christians build houses illegally and are discovered, they are given licenses to build after the fact, and are not significantly fined.

A villager in the village of Mavromati outside of Komotini told Helsinki Watch that his house, which he is building illegally, had cost him 100,000 drachmas to build so far. "Then I was fined 150,000 drachmas, and the house isn't even finished yet. It has no door, and so I can't live in it. At every step, I have to pay another fine."

Ahmet Haciosman, an imam in Komotini, told Helsinki Watch that there are illegally-constructed buildings in virtually every town in Greece. "In 1985 or 1986," he said, "a decision was made that every illegal building would be made legal and incorporated into town plans. But there were two exceptions: Athens and Western Thrace -- Athens because they didn't want Athens to become any larger, and Western Thrace because the Turkish minority lives here."

Ismail Molla Rodoplu, a former Parliamentarian, told Helsinki Watch that there are about 100 families without water or electricity in Komotini, living in illegal houses.

Xanthi Nomark Thanopolous reported that there are many out-of-plan, or illegal houses in his area, many "built in pre-election periods to avoid police investigations. Three months ago, I tried to transfer my authority to license illegal buildings to the heads of those communities, but the Ministry for Buildings and Plans would not allow it."

Land is of major importance in Western Thrace, which is largely a farming area; tobacco is one of the most important crops. Villagers in Mavromati reported that they cannot buy land, but asserted that the government gives land to Greek Christians at no cost. "The grazing land that belongs to our village has been given by the government to Christian villagers," one villager said.

**Expropriation of Land:** Members of the Turkish community also complained about the government's expropriation of land in Western Thrace; they allege that land is frequently confiscated from Greek Turks, but only rarely from other Greeks. In 1978 the government confiscated between 3,000 and 4,000 acres to build the University of Thrace on the outskirts of Komotini; only a small portion of the area has been used for about twenty school buildings. Many tobacco farmers and other families were dispossessed and, as a result, emigrated to Turkey. The villagers told Helsinki Watch that they had offered the government 500 acres free of charge if the government would not confiscate the rest of the land, but that the offer had been refused.

According to information provided to Helsinki Watch by Greek Information Office Director Nikos Papaconstantinou, "for the establishment of the University schools in Komotini, 85% of the appropriated land belonged to Moslems, while for the establishment of the equivalent university school in Xanthi, 82% of the appropriated land belonged to Christians. The allegations regarding a discriminatory Greek land policy against the Thracian Moslems have no scientific base whatsoever."

The Turkish community reports that between 1976 and 1980 the government confiscated 3,000 acres for an industrial area -- for factories, about eight kilometers from Komotini -- and that ninety percent of this land was taken from ethnic Turks. It alleges that the government deliberately chose the best land to take for the technical area, a process that they say had not been done in areas being developed in Kavala, a good-sized city west of Xanthi, in the province of Macedonia. Around 1980, ethnic Turks report, the government expropriated 1,500 acres to use for homes for Pontic Greeks who were coming to Greece from the Soviet Union. About 100 Pontic Greek families live there now, in new modern houses with a new modern school.

Helsinki Watch was told that the government has recently been discussing expropriating 6,000 acres of very fertile land owned by the Turkish community in Sappe near Komotini for use as an open-air prison. The Turkish minority believes that this would be another disaster, forcing thousands of farmers to migrate to Turkey. Although the owners would be paid for the land, they would not be permitted to buy other land or to buy or build commercial buildings with the money.

In the village of Evlalon, outside of Xanthi, a villager told Helsinki Watch that the government was trying to take 3,000 acres of his farm land, claiming that it is government land, although he has papers and a map from the Ottoman Empire showing that the land is his. The case has been in court for eight years.

In some instances, the Turkish community reports, the Greek government has confiscated land and then leased it back to ethnic Turks, who then continue to farm it.

**Business and Professional Life**: The Turkish minority claims that the practice of denying Greek Turks permission to buy houses and land, or to build or repair houses or mosques, pertains also to businesses. Permission from the Nomark's office is required to buy or sell businesses; as a result, there are reportedly no Turkish-owned factories, gas stations or pharmacies. Ethnic Turks say that they can work in stores, or rent facilities for stores, but that they can never become partners with other Greek citizens, or start new large businesses, or buy stores. Ali Muminoglu, a mechanical engineer in Xanthi who is the technical director of a marble factory, told Helsinki Watch that he has been trying for many years to get permission to build a factory. He says that the Nomark's office has told him he can obtain permission, but continues to put him off, telling him to wait another ten days or a month and that the office will not give him his file number, without which he cannot take legal action. A baker in Xanthi told Helsinki Watch that he was able to rent space for his pastry shop, but had been trying for several years without any success to get permission to buy new machinery.

Ibrahim Salihoglu, the owner of a small grocery store in the village of Filira, received a license for his store in 1978. In 1987, Salihoglu wanted to enlarge his shop from 30 to 40 square meters. Local police told him he would need a new license to do so, but the Nomark's office in Komotini told him he did not need one. However, the local police threatened to close his shop if he tried to enlarge it without a new license (see Appendix F), took him to the police station and detained him for 24 hours. Mr. Salihoglu has not been able to enlarge his store.

**Licenses**: Greek Turks assert that they are rarely permitted to obtain licenses to drive tractors needed for farming. Mechanical engineer Ali Muminoglu told Helsinki Watch that over 3,000 applications for tractor drivers' licenses had been denied in Western Thrace in recent years. According to Turkish consul Alpmen, tractor licenses are nearly impossible to obtain. Ordinary driver's licenses can also be difficult to acquire; some ethnic Turks report that you must know someone or bribe someone to get a driver's license.

Xanthi Nomark Thanopolous, on the other hand, told Helsinki Watch that any problems in obtaining driver's licenses were due to language problems; that many Moslems did not want to learn Greek, and therefore were unable to get licenses.

The Turkish community reports that ethnic Turkish professional people are also denied the opportunities available to other Greeks. One example given to Helsinki Watch is a pharmacist in Komotini who has a diploma from the Ministry of Health in Athens and has been trying since 1982 to get permission from the Nomark to open a pharmacy. Another example is Dr. Sadik Ahmet, who is a surgeon, trained in a Greek medical school in Thessaloniki. Dr. Ahmet told Helsinki Watch that when he applied for a hospital position (a government job) in Komotini in 1984, there was one open spot for a surgeon, and only one applicant--Dr. Sadik. The hospital refused his application and filled the position two months later with a Greek Christian. Dr. Ahmet said that he was told that he should, instead, find a position in a hospital in Thessaloniki.

Nomark Thanopolous of Xanthi, however, told Helsinki Watch that licenses are routinely given to open pharmacies, but that one application is pending because of problems with the documents. He said that no applications are pending to build factories or to buy machinery for pastry shops.

According to Nomark Karahalios of Komotini, Greek Moslems can buy gas stations and stores, and build factories.

**Civil Service Jobs**: Greek Turks say they are denied opportunities to work in civil service jobs; they report that ethnic Turks hold three or four jobs as street cleaners for municipal governments, but no higher-level positions. Of the 300 employees in the Komotini Nomark's office,

Nomark Karaholios told Helsinki Watch that none are of Turkish origin. He said that no Turks had applied, because most worked in agriculture. Of the 1,000 civil servants in the Xanthi Nomark's office, Nomark Thanapolous told Helsinki Watch that none are ethnic Turks. He, too, said that none had applied. He said this was because "Most Moslems marry young, have many children, and work in agriculture and in private services. So they don't want to go into public service. Partly it's because of their difficulties with the Greek language."

A group of Greek Turks in Xanthi told Helsinki Watch they did not know the total number of applicants for civil service jobs, and acknowledged that some qualified people no longer apply, knowing that they will be denied. However, they provided the names of six educated ethnic Turks who had applied to the Xanthi Nomark's office for positions in recent years:

- Mehmet Raifoglu, a dentist, who applied in 1989;

- Ramadan Duban, an economist, who applied in 1989;

- Mehmet Molaserifhasan, a graduate of a teaching academy, who applied in 1988;

- Halil Ethem, a pharmacist, who applied in 1985 and 1986, and has now gone to Turkey;

- Cavi Tungur, a pharmacist, who applied in 1985; and

- Yuksel Nurioglu, a pharmacist, who has been applying since 1982; his case has now gone to the High Court in Athens.[21]

None of the six had obtained jobs through the Nomark's office.

---

[21] See Appendix G for a copy of Nurioglu's university certificate that indicates that he is qualified to open a pharmacy anywhere in Greece. Helsinki Watch was shown documents indicating that Nurioglu's file had been lost on each of the three attempts he made to obtain permission to open a pharmacy.

According to member of Parliament Faikoglu, the Greek government has had a policy since 1985 of hiring ethnic Turks for civil service jobs in other parts of Greece--in Kavala, or Athens--but only if the Turk is willing to leave Western Thrace, taking his family with him, and vote in his new location.

**Credit**: Greek Turks report that they cannot get credit from Greek banks, although other Greeks can. Villagers in Mavromati told Helsinki Watch that they cannot get the bank loans they need to farm their land. Men in the village of Ziloti said that, although they often applied for bank credit, they were not able to secure it.

Dr. Sadik Ahmet told Helsinki Watch that in a decision dated November 22, 1966, the three government banks, including the agricultural bank and the national bank, agreed to give credit to Greek Christians to buy Turkish land or Turkish houses in Western Thrace. The credit was good for twenty years and could be used only to buy Turkish land and houses; if the money was used for something else, the government would take back the credit. Dr. Ahmet said that no such credit was given to the Turkish community.

**Schools**: Schools are an issue of great concern to the Turkish community. Article 40 of the Lausanne Treaty provides that the Turkish minority shall have

> an equal right to establish, manage and control at their own expense . . . any schools and other establishments for instruction and education, with the right to use their own language and to exercise their own religion freely therein.

In spite of this international agreement, Greek Turks report that they are unable to build new schools or to repair old ones, that they are not permitted to appoint their own Turkish teachers, and that their children are taught with old, out-dated Turkish-language schoolbooks. Ethnic Turkish children between the ages of seven and twelve attend their own elementary schools, where they are taught in both Turkish and Greek. According to Dr. Sadik Ahmet, about 70 percent of the schoolbooks are in the Greek language; twenty years ago, only 20 percent were in Greek. He studied geography and history in Turkish; his son studies them in Greek. Members of the Turkish minority told Helsinki Watch that it used to appoint its own teachers, but that now both Turkish and Greek teachers are appointed by the Greek government. The Turkish-language teachers are trained in a special academy in Thessaloniki; the Turkish community believes that many of the teachers do not speak Turkish well and are inferior teachers. The Turkish community reports that there are 250 Turkish elementary schools in Western Thrace, with about 12,000 students, but there are only two Turkish secondary schools, one in Xanthi and one in Komotini.[23] Each of the secondary schools takes 140 or 150 students. An entrance exam in Greek determines which students will be admitted to the Turkish secondary schools. Helsinki Watch was told that, as a result, many ethnic Turkish children are sent to Turkey for secondary school education; Dr. Ahmet estimated that 270 such children went to Turkey in 1989. According to Mr. Onder Alpmen, the Turkish consul in Komotini, fewer than ten percent of the students who graduate from Turkish elementary schools attend Greek secondary schools. He believes that about 70 percent of elementary school graduates go to Turkey to attend secondary school.

According to a "position paper" released by the Greek government in connection with the trial of Dr. Sadik and Mr. Serif and provided to Helsinki Watch by Greek Information Office Director Papaconstantinou, the minority secondary schools

> were established and financed by the Greek authorities to improve the educational standards of Moslem pupils. Obviously it is out of the question for Greece to allow Greek students, whether Moslems or Christians, to continue higher education without possessing the fundamentals of the Greek language which, unfortunately, is the case among the majority of Moslem pupils. This is the main reason for the establishment of the entrance exams in the two Turkish secondary schools. . . [A] substantial effort is being made by the Greek government to improve the teaching of Greek in the primary schools.

Helsinki Watch visited elementary schools in Komotini and in the villages of Ziloti, outside of Komotini, and Zigos, outside of Xanthi. The

---

[23] According to Greek Information Office Director Papaconstantinou, there are 300 primary schools, two Moslem religious schools, two secular high schools and four gymnasiums serving the Moslem minority in Western Thrace.

Komotini school was in a large building that needed repairs. Each of the village schools was in a small building in disrepair. In Ziloti, 25 children, ages 6 through 12, were taught in a two-room schoolhouse by one Greek and one Turkish teacher.

In Zigos, the school shared a building with the mosque, as the old school had collapsed, and village leaders said they had not received permission to build a new one. Teacher Mehmet Sirkeci teaches 25 children between the ages of 6 and 12 in one room on the ground floor; grades 4, 5 and 6 are taught by another teacher in a room upstairs. Mr. Sirkeci said that there were two Greek schools in the village; one was in a new building in which twelve children were being taught.

Mr. Terifih Huseyinoglu, a teacher in the Xanthi secondary school, told Helsinki Watch that almost none of the students who graduated from his school went on to Greek universities because the entrance examinations in Greek were very difficult.

**Schoolbooks**: Again and again, members of the Turkish community complained to Helsinki Watch about the schoolbooks used by their children in elementary schools. Mr. Musa Ferit, in the village of Ziloti, for example, reported that his grandchildren were reading the same books he had read in primary school, with 20- to 40-year-old technology, torn and missing pages, and statements like, "someday man will be able to visit the moon." Dr. Sadik Ahmet also reported that his son was using the same schoolbooks he had used in 1960.

In visits to elementary schools, our examination of schoolbooks corroborated these complaints: the Greek textbooks were new; the Turkish textbooks were old and worn, dating from 1970 or earlier, frequently with pages missing.

The question of textbooks has apparently been caught up in the enmity between Greece and Turkey. The cultural accord signed by Greece and Turkey in 1968 (referred to earlier in the section on Greece's obligations under international law) states that each country must provide the other with samples of the schoolbooks to be used. According to the Turkish consul in Komotini, Mr. Alpmen, Turkish books were given to the Greek authorities for their approval in 1978. At first, he said, Greek authorities approved the books, but later did not permit the Turkish minority to distribute them. Greece then required changes in the books-- such things as changing from Turkish cities to Greek cities in math problems asking the distance between cities, and changing math problems from calculations in Turkish lira to Greek drachmas. No substantive changes were required. According to Mr. Alpmen, new books were prepared with the changes asked by the Greek authorities, but the books have still not been approved.

On May 14, 1990, Dr. Sadik Ahmet met with Greek Prime Minister Constantine Mitsotakis to discuss the problems of the Turkish minority, including the schoolbook matter. According to Greek government sources, as reported in *Dateline*, May 19, 1990, the Prime Minister told Dr. Ahmet that the schoolbook problem was the fault of Turkey, not Greece. He said that under the terms of the Lausanne Treaty, schoolbooks are supposed by be specially adapted for use by Greek nationals who are members of the Turkish minority. But he said that the requested changes had never been made by Turkish educational authorities, and that Turkey had been sending to Greece the same textbooks used in primary grades in Turkey. Greek authorities object to those textbooks, he said, because they are intended to educate the children as if they were citizens of Turkey.

## Recommendations

Helsinki Watch recommends that the Greek government:

Abide by its obligations under international and national law to protect the Turkish minority's human rights; specifically, to:

o   Acknowledge the existence of the Turkish minority and grant them all the civil and political rights enjoyed by other Greek citizens; this should include the right to call themselves and their associations and schools "Turkish;"

o   Accord the Turkish minority the freedom to leave Greece and return, without the threat of deprivation of citizenship; accord freedom of movement within Greece;

o   Guarantee the Turkish minority equal rights, in policy and practice, to buy and sell land and houses, to build, enlarge and repair houses, schools and mosques;

o   Guarantee the Turkish minority equal rights in business and professional life and equal access to civil service employment;

o   Accord the Turkish minority freedom of expression, including access to radio, television and publications from Turkey; end the harassment of the Turkish minority press;

o   Enforce international agreements forbidding degrading treatment of the Turkish minority, including harassment by Greek authorities;

o   Provide the Turkish minority with freedom of religion, including the selection of muftis and the control of religious endowments;

o  Accord to the Turkish minority the right to build, enlarge and repair its schools, to appoint its Turkish-language teachers, and to obtain and use current schoolbooks in the Turkish language.

Helsinki Watch recommends that the United States government, in light of its long friendship with Greece and its continuing provision of military assistance ($348,495,000 for Fiscal Year 1990), acknowledge and condemn the human rights abuses documented in this report, and use its best efforts to persuade the government of Greece to carry out the recommendations listed above.

# Appendix A

**Convention Concerning the Exchange of Greek and Turkish Populations.**
**Signed at Lausanne, January 30, 1923.**

The Government of the Grand National Assembly of Turkey and the Greek Government have agreed upon the following provisions:

Article 1.

As from the 1st May, 1923, there shall take place a compulsory exchange of Turkish nationals of the Greek Orthodox religion established in Turkish territory, and of Greek nationals of the Moslem religion established in Greek territory.

These persons shall not return to live in Turkey or Greece respectively without the authorisation of the Turkish Government or of the Greek Government respectively.

Article 2.

The following persons shall not be included in the exchange provided for in Article 1:
   a) The Greek inhabitants of Constantinople
   b) The Moslem inhabitants of Western Thrace.

All Greeks who were already established before the 30th October, 1918, within the areas under the Prefecture of the City of Constantinople, as defined by the law of 1912, shall be considered as Greek inhabitants of Constantinople.

All Moslems established in the region to the east of the frontier line laid down in 1913 by the Treaty of Bucharest shall be considered as Moslem inhabitants of Western Thrace.

Article 3.

Those Greeks and Moslems who have already, and since the 18th October, 1912, left the territories the Greek and Turkish inhabitants of which are to be respectively exchanged, shall be considered as included in the exchange provided for in Article 1.

The expression "emigrant" in the present Convention includes all physical and juridical persons who have been obliged to emigrate or have emigrated since the 18th October, 1912.

Article 4.

All able-bodied men belonging to the Greek population, whose families have already left Turkish territory, and who are now detained in Turkey, shall constitute the first installment of Greeks sent to Greece in accordance with the present Convention.

# Appendix B

## Treaty of Lausanne

Section III. Protection of Minorities

Article 37.

Turkey undertakes that the stipulations contained in Articles 38 to 44 shall be recognised as fundamental laws, and that no law, no regulation, nor official action shall conflict or interfere with these stipulations, nor shall any law, regulation, nor official action prevail over them.

Article 38.

The Turkish Government undertakes to assure full and complete protection of life and liberty to all inhabitants of Turkey without distinction of birth, nationality, language, race or religion.

All inhabitants of Turkey shall be entitled to free exercise, whether in public or private, of any creed, religion or belief, the observance of which shall not be incompatible with public order and good morals.

Non-Moslem minorities will enjoy full freedom of movement and of emigration, subject to the measures applied, on the whole or on part of the territory, to all Turkish nationals, and which may be taken by the Turkish Government for national defence, or for the maintenance of public order.

Article 39.

Turkish nationals belonging to non-Moslem minorities will enjoy the same civil and political rights as Moslems.

All the inhabitants of Turkey, without distinction of religion, shall be equal before the law.

Differences of religion, creed or confession shall not prejudice any Turkish national in matters relating to the enjoyment of civil or political rights, as, for instance, admission to public employments, functions and honours, or the exercise of professions and industries.

No restrictions shall be imposed on the free use by any Turkish national of any language in private intercourse, in commerce, religion, in the press, or in publications of any kind or at public meetings.

Notwithstanding the existence of the official language, adequate facilities shall be given to Turkish nationals of non-Turkish speech for the oral use of their own language before the Courts.

Article 40.

Turkish nationals belonging to non-Moslem minorities shall enjoy the same treatment and security in law and in fact as other Turkish nationals. In particular, they shall have an equal right to establish, manage and control at their own expense, any charitable, religious and social institutions, any schools and other establishments for instruction and education, with the right to use their own language and to exercise their own religion freely therein.

Article 41.

As regards public instruction, the Turkish Government will grant in those towns and districts, where a considerable proportion of non-Moslem nationals are resident, adequate facilities for ensuring that in the primary schools the instruction shall be given to the children of such Turkish nationals through the medium of their own language. This provision will not prevent the Turkish Government from making the teaching of the Turkish language obligatory in the said schools.

In towns and districts where there is a considerable proportion of Turkish nationals belonging to non-Moslem minorities, these minorities shall be assured an equitable share in the enjoyment and application of the sums which may be provided out of public funds under the State, municipal, or other budgets for educational, religious, or charitable purposes.

The sums in question shall be paid to the qualified representatives of the establishments and institutions concerned.

Article 42.

The Turkish Government undertakes to take, as regards non-Moslem minorities, in so far as concerns their family law or personal status, measures permitting the settlement of these questions in accordance with the customs of those minorities,

These measures will be elaborated by special Commissions composed of representatives of the Turkish Government and of representatives of each of the minorities concerned in equal number. In case of divergence, the Turkish Government and the Council of the League of Nations will appoint in agreement an umpire chosen from amongst European lawyers.

The Turkish Government undertakes to grant full protection to the churches, synagogues, cemeteries, and other religious establishments of the above-mentioned minorities. All facilities and authorisation will be granted to the pious foundations, and to the religious and charitable institutions of the said minorities at present existing in Turkey, and the Turkish Government will not refuse, for the formation of new religious and charitable institutions, any of the necessary facilities which are guaranteed to other private institutions of that nature.

Article 43.

Turkish nationals belonging to non-Moslem minorities shall not be compelled to perform any act which constitutes a violation of their faith or religious observances, and shall not be placed under any disability by reason of their refusal to attend Courts of Law or to perform any legal business on their weekly day of rest.

This provision, however, shall not exempt such Turkish nationals from such obligations as shall be imposed upon all other Turkish nationals for the preservation of public order.

Article 44.

Turkey agrees that, in so far as the preceding Articles of this Section affect non-Moslem nationals of Turkey, these provisions constitute obligations of international concern and shall be placed under the guarantee of the League of Nations. They shall not be modified without the assent of the majority of the Council of the League of Nations. The British Empire, France, Italy and Japan hereby agree not to withhold their assent to any modification in these Articles which is in due form assented to by a majority of the Council of the League of Nations.

Turkey agrees that any Member of the Council of the League of Nations shall have the right to bring to the attention of the Council any infraction or danger of infraction of any of these obligations, and that the Council may thereupon take such action and give such directions as it may deem proper and effective in the circumstances.

Turkey further agrees that any difference of opinion as to questions of law or of fact arising out of these Articles between the Turkish Government and any one of the other Signatory Powers or any other Power, a member of the Council of the League of Nations, shall be held to be a dispute of an international character under Article 14 of the Covenant of the League of Nations. The Turkish Government hereby consents that any such dispute shall, if the other party thereto demands, be referred to the Permanent Court of International Justice. The decision of the Permanent Court shall be final and shall have the same force and effect as an award under Article 13 of the Covenant.

Article 45.

The rights conferred by the provisions of the present Section on the non-Moslem minorities of Turkey will be similarly conferred by Greece on the Moslem minority in her territory.

# Appendix C

ΒΑΣΙΛΕΙΟΝ ΤΗΣ ΕΛΛΑΔΟΣ
ΓΕΝΙΚΗ ΔΙΟΙΚΗΣΙΣ ΘΡΑΚΗΣ
ΔΙΕΥΘΥΝΣΙΣ ΕΣΩΤΕΡΙΚΩΝ
Αρ:θ: Πρωτ. Α1043
Εν Κομοτηνή τη 27/12/1954
ΕΠΕΙΓΟΥΣΑ
Προς
τους κ.κ Δημάρχους και Προέδρους Κοινοτήτων Ν. Ροδόπης. Κατόπιν διαταγής του κ. Προέδρου της Κυβερνήσεως, παρακαλούμεν όπως εφεξής εις πάσαν περίπτωσιν γίνεται χρήσις του όρου «Τούρκος - Τουρκικό» αντί του τοιούτου «Μουσουλμάνας-Μουσουλμανικό».

Ο Γενικό Διοικητής Θράκης
Γ. Φεσσόπουλος

Türkçesi:
«Sayın Hükümet Başkanının emri üzerine bundan böyle gereken her yerde «Müslüman-Müslümanca» deyimleri yerine «Türk-Türkçe» deyimlerini kullanmanızı rica ederiz.»

Trakya Genel Valisi
G. Fessopulos

Translation:
Kingdom of Greece
General Administration of Thraka
Interior Office
Number of Protocol A1043

Komotene, 27/12/1954

URGENT

TO: The Mayors and Presidents of the Communes of the Prefecture of Rodope.

Following the order of the President of the Government (Prime Minister) we ask you that from now on and in all occasions the terms "Turk-Turkish" are used instead of the terms "Muslim- of Muslim".

The General Administrator
of Thraka

G. Fessopoulos

ΔΙΕΥΘΥΝΣΙΣ ΕΣΩΤΕΡΙΚΩΝ
Αριθμ/Πρωτ. Α202

Εν Κομοτηνή τη 5)2)1955

Παρά τας αυστηράς διαταγάς της κυβερνήσεως περί της αντικαταστάσεως και χρησιμοποιήσεως του λοιπού, των όρων «Μουσουλμάνος -Μουσουλμανικός» διά των τοιούτων «Τούρκος – Τουρκικός» εις το χωρίον Άρατος επί της δημοσίας οδού Κομοτηνής – Αλεξανδρουπόλεως, υφίσταται επιγραφή, εμφανεστάτη, αναγράφουσα «Μουσουλμανικόν Σχολείον».

Να αντικατασταθεί, αμέσως, τόσον αυτή, όσον και πάσα άλλη τυχόν υπάρχουσα εις την περιοχήν του Νομού Ροδόπης.

Ο Γεν. Διοικητής Θράκης
Γ. Φεσσόπουλος

«Bundan böyle «Müslüman-Müslümanca» deyimleri yerine: «Türk-Türkçe» deyimlerinin kullanılmasına ilişkin Hükümetin sert emirlerine rağmen, Komotini - Aleksandrupolis milli yolu üzerindeki Aratos köyünde «Müslüman Okulu» başlıklı bir tabelâ cok seçik bir şekilde halâ mevcut bulunmaktadır.

Gerek bu, gerekse Rodop ili bölgesinde muhtemelen mevcut olan tüm benzeri tabelâlar derhal değiştirilmelidir.»

Trakya Genel Valisi
G. Fessopulos

Translation:
Kingdom of Greece
General Administration of Thraka
Interior Office
Number of Protocol A202

Komotene, 5/2/1955

In spite of the strict orders of the government to replace the terms "Muslim-of Muslim" and use from now on the terms "Turk-Turkish", in the village Aratos on the public road connecting Komotene and Alexandroupole there exists a very prominent sign with the words "Muslim School".

It, as well as any other such signs that might exist in the area of the Prefecture of Rodope, should be replaced immediately.

The General Administrator
of Thraka

G. Fessopoulos

## Appendix D

### Summons of 8 February 1990

The prosecutor of the criminal courts in Rodopi, in conformity with articles 245, 320, and 321 of the Penal Code, invites the son of Ahmet, Mr. Sadik Ahmet Sadik residing at H. Trikupi Avenue No: 83, Komotini, to be present at the three member (judges) criminal court of Rodopi on 8 February 1990, for trial.

He has violated article 192 of the Penal Code, in the town of Komotini and elsewhere within the prefect of Rodopi on 17 November, 1989. The said article stipulates the imprisonment of up to two years, unless a stiffer penalty is specified by another article, those who openly or otherwise disrupt the public peace by inciting violence and division among the citizens. It is based on the evidence that the defendant has published and undersigned a declaration in the newspaper "Guven" on 17 November, 1989 in which he made false assertions to the effect that the Greek authorities discriminated against and oppressed the Thracian Muslims. Referred to the Muslim minority in Thrace as a Turkish minority instead of using the term "Hellenic Muslim Minority", thereby inciting division among the citizens, particularly between the Muslim citizens eventually disrupting public peace among the citizens in Thrace.

Consequently he has violated articles 14/1, 26/1-A, 27/1 and 192 of the Penal Code.

Komotini, 18 December 1989

Prosecutor
Seal and Signature
(Panagiotis Mentzas)

# Appendix E

ΕΛΛΗΝΙΚΗ ΔΗΜΟΚΡΑΤΙΑ
ΝΟΜΑΡΧΙΑ ΡΟΔΟΠΗΣ

Κομοτηνή  4- 2- 1985
Αριθ. πρωτ.: ΤΠΠΕ 2II

ΔΙΕΥΘΥΝΣΗ Πολεοδομίας και
ΤΜΗΜΑ Πολεοδομικών Εφαρμογών
Ταχ. Δ/νση: Διοικητήριο
Ταχ. κώδικος:
Πληροφορίες: Γραφείο Εκδόσ. Αδειών
Τηλέφωνο: 26582/38I εσωτ.

ΠΡΟΣ: Τον κ. Ομέρ Χοτζά Ραήφ
Πρόεδρο της Διαχ/κής Επιτροπής
του Μουσουλμανικού Τεμένους
του χωρίου Συμβόλων
Σύμβολα

ΚΟΙΝ.: Αθανάσιο Σουρή Πολ/κό Μηχ/κό
Λεωφ. Ηρώων 7    Κομοτηνή

ΘΕΜΑ: Επιστρέφεται φάκελλος μελέτης επισκευής του Μουσουλμανικού Τεμένους στα σύμβολα.
Σχετ. Το με αριθ. πρωτ. 94755/π.ε./I4-9-I984 έγγραφό μας

    Σε συνέχεια με το παραπάνω σχετικό έγγραφό μας με το οποίο σας είχαμε γνωρίσει τις ελλείψεις που παρουσιάζει ο φάκελλος μελέτης επισκευής Τεμένους που υποβάλατε στην Υπηρεσία μας για την έκδοση σχετικής αδείας και κατόπιν της ταυτάριθμης αίτησής σας με την οποία υποβάλατε μόνον τοπογραφικό διάγραμμα του οικοπέδου, φωτογραφίες και δήλωση του Ν. Δ/τος I05/69 σας επιστρέφουμε το φάκελλο γιατί αν και παρήλθε διάστημα πλέον των τεσσάρων (4) μηνών από την σχετική ειδοποίηση μας σεις δεν επιδείξατε το ανάλογο ενδιαφέρον για να συμπληρωθεί ο φάκελλος μελέτης με όλα τα απαραίτητα δικαιολογητικά.
Ακόμη σας πληροφορούμε ότι σε περίπτωση που θέλετε να επανυποβάλετε σχετική αίτηση για την χορήγηση αδείας επισκευής του Τεμένους Συμβόλων θα πρέπει η σχετική μελέτη να συνταχθεί σύμφωνα με τις προδιαγραφές του Πρ. Δ/τος 3/9/I983 (ΦΕΚ 394 Δ/8-9-83) και να υποβάλετε εκτός των άλλων δικαιολογητικών και α) Οδοιπορικό διάγραμμα του οικοπέδου και της περιοχής β) Αναλυτικός προϋπολογισμός των εργασιών βάσει ΑΤΟΕ γ) τίτλους ιδιοκτησίας και πρόσφατο πιστοποιητικό ιδιοκτησίας και δ) Έγκριση της Ιεράς Μητροπόλεως Μαρωνείας Κομοτηνής.-

Συνημμένα
Φάκελλος προς επιστροφή

Ο Προϊστάμενος του
Τ.Π. και Π.Ε.

ΠΙΣΤΟ ΑΝΤΙΓΡΑΦΟ

Στέλιος Ματανάς
Αρχ/χτων με 4ο β

Translation:

Komotene, 4-2-1985

The Hellenic Republic
Prefecture of Rodope

Number of Protocol (not legible)

Office: Office of Town-Planning and Town-Planning Projects
Post Office
Address: Administration Office
Information: Office of Permit Approvals
Telephone: 26582/381 ext.

To: Mr. Omer Hotza Raef
President of the Managing Committee of the Muslim Temple in the village of Sembola
Sembola

Also sent to: Athansios Koures
Civil Engineer
7 Heroon Ave.
Komotene

Re: The return of the planning file regarding restoration of the Muslim Temple in Sembola. In relation to our letter with number of protocol 94755/??/14-9-1984

  Following up on the aforementioned letter with which we informed you of the deficiencies present in the planning file for the restoration of the Muslim Temple that you submitted to our Office for approval of the required permit, and given the application, under the same number, that you submitted presenting only the topographic diagram of the building plot, photographs and the form required by the statute 105/69, we return to you the file because even though a period of more than four (4) months has elapsed since our notification on that matter you failed to show the appropriate interest in completing the planning file with the necessary documents.
  We also inform you that in the case you wish to reapply for the permit approval for the restoration of the Temple in Sembola the plan would have to be compiled according to the specifications of the Presidential Decree 3/9/1983 (FEK 394 D/8-9-83) and you must submit

beyond the other documents also a) a detailed diagram of the building-plot and the nearby area b) detailed budget of the works according to ATOE c) titles of the property and recent titles of ownership and d) approval of the Holy Cathedral of Maronea - Komotene.

Enclosed
File to be returned

Person in Charge

Stelios Matanas
Architect 4

Γ.Κ.
ΕΛΛΗΝΙΚΗ ΔΗΜΟΚΡΑΤΙΑ
ΕΛΛΗΝΙΚΗ ΑΣΤΥΝΟΜΙΑ
ΑΣΤΥΝ. ΤΜΗΜΑ ΤΑΞΕΩΣ
Φ Ι Λ Υ Ρ Α Σ
ΑΡΙΘ. ΠΡΩΤ: 1020/4830/21

## Appendix F

Φιλύρα 9 Ιουλίου 1987

ΘΕΜΑ: "Περί κλεισίματος καταστήματος του ΣΑΛΗ ΟΓΛΟΥ Ιμπραήμ του Σαλή και της Γκιουλσούμ, γεν. το 1926 στο Δειλινό - Ροδόπης, κατοίκου ομοίως".-

Παρακαλούμε όπως εντός 4 ημερών από σήμερα αποσύρατε τα ευαλοίωτα είδη του καταστήματός σας, γιατί λειτουργεί χωρίς άδεια της αρμοδίας αρχής, καθ'όσον έχετε κάνει επέκταση της ήδη υπαρχούσης αδείας λειτουργίας καταστήματός σας και θα προβούμε στο κλείσιμο αυτού δια σφραγίσεως.-

Ο
Διοικητής του Τμήματος
ΧΑΤΖΗΠΑΝΑΓΙΩΤΗΣ
Ανθυπαστυνόμος Β΄

### Translation:

**The Hellenic Republic**
**The Hellenic Police**
**Police Precinct of Felera**
**Number of Protocol: 1020/4830/21**

Felera, 9 July 1987

Re: "For the closing of the store of Sale Oglou Ebraem of Sale and Gioulsoum, born in 1926 in Delena of Rodope, residing in the same place."

We ask you that within 4 days from today you have removed the perishable goods from your store because it is operated without the permission of the authorities, since you have extended the existing permit of operation for your store so we will close it and seal it.

The Commanding Officer

Hatzipanagiotes

**Appendix G**

ΕΛΛΗΝΙΚΗ ΔΗΜΟΚΡΑΤΙΑ

ΑΡΙΘ. ΠΡΩΤ. 1598
ΔΙΕΚΠ. 161

# ΑΝΩΤΑΤΟΝ ΥΓΕΙΟΝΟΜΙΚΟΝ ΣΥΜΒΟΥΛΙΟΝ

Ὁ Κος _Γουζέλ Μαυρή Μαυρπούζου ἐν ξάνθης_ ὑποστὰς τὴν νενομισμένην δοκιμασίαν ἐνώπιον τοῦ Ἀνωτάτου Ὑγειονομικοῦ Συμβουλίου ἔλαβε τὴν ἄδειαν μετὰ τοῦ βαθμοῦ _ἄριστα_ ἵνα μετέρχεται ἐν Ἑλλάδι τὴν Φαρμακευτικήν, τηρῶν τοὺς νόμους τοῦ Κράτους.

Ἐν Ἀθήναις τῇ 25-1-1982

Ο ΠΡΟΕΔΡΟΣ

ΤΑ ΜΕΛΗ

Ο ΓΡΑΜΜΑΤΕΥΣ

ΕΠΙΚΥΡΟΥΤΑΙ

Ἐν Ἀθήναις τῇ 28-4-1982

Ο ΥΠΟΥΡΓΟΣ

ΠΑΡ. ΑΥΓΕΡΙΝΟΣ